WALKABOUT
Weather

This edition 2003

Franklin Watts
96 Leonard Street
London EC2A 4XD

Franklin Watts Australia
45-51 Huntley Street
Alexandria
NSW 2015

Copyright © 1993 Franklin Watts
Editor: Ambreen Husain
Design: Volume One

A CIP catalogue record for this book is available from
the British Library.
Dewey Decimal Classification Number: 551.6

ISBN: 0 7496 5267 5

Printed in Hong Kong/China

Photographs: Bruce Coleman Ltd (J Fry) 5,
(G Ahrens) 19, (C James) 22; Eye Ubiquitous
(D Fobister) 30; Chris Fairclough Colour Library
5 inset, 10; Robert Harding 9, (G White) 20, 27, 28;
Hutchison Library (B Regent) 14 inset; Frank Lane
Picture Agency (M Nimmo) 11, (D Jones) 15,
(G Nystrand) 17, (E & D Hosking) 26; Oxford
Scientific Films (E Robinson) 8; Science Photo
Library (C & M Perennou) 14; Swift Picture Library
(M Read) 6, 7, (G Dore) 21; ZEFA 4, 12-13, 16, 18, 23,
24, 25, 29, 31.

WALKABOUT
Weather

Henry Pluckrose

FRANKLIN WATTS
LONDON • SYDNEY

Have you ever thought
how different the weather
can be?
In summer time
the days are warm.

In winter time
the days are often cold.
We measure how hot
or how cold it is
with a thermometer.
A thermometer measures
temperature.

If the weather is very dry
and very hot
the sun dries up rivers
and ponds.
The soil cracks.
Plants cannot grow
without water.

Sometimes if there is
too much rain
rivers overflow their banks.
Floods can cause a lot
of damage.

In very cold weather
water freezes.
Ponds and rivers are covered
with a thin skin of ice.
Animals and birds die
if they cannot find food.
The most pleasant days
are those when
it is not too hot
and not too cold.

What sort of weather
is this?
Very wet!

Clouds like these bring rain.
When dark clouds pile up
there may be a storm.

Each cloud is made up of tiny drops of water. These drops of water join up and become larger and heavier. Heavy drops of water fall to the ground... as rain.

Roofs, roads and fields
do not stay wet…
however hard the rain.
The sun warms the water
in puddles, ponds, rivers
and seas.
The water changes
into water vapour.
This damp air rises.
As it cools
it turns into
tiny drops of water
which form clouds.

If it is very cold
the water in the clouds
turns to ice.
The ice crystals join up
into six-pointed snowflakes.
These snowflakes fall
from the clouds.
If they stay cold
they fall as snow.

Sometimes the rain freezes
as it falls.
Hailstones are tiny balls of ice.

When it is very cold
hoar frost forms on
the ground and on plants…

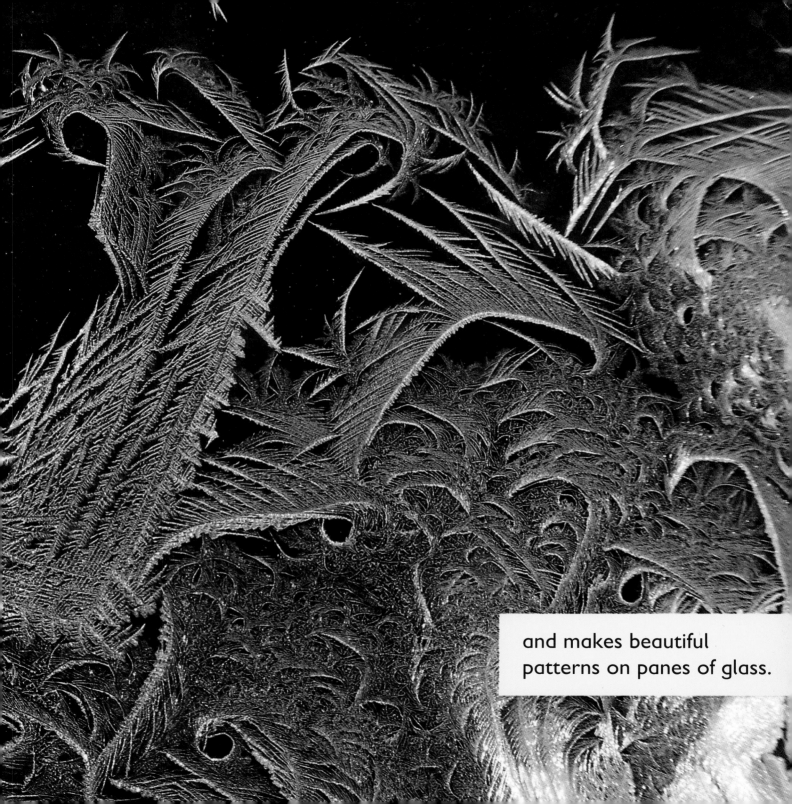

and makes beautiful
patterns on panes of glass.

If you look up
at clouds
you will notice that they
are moving.
Winds blow them across the sky.
Wind is moving air.

You cannot see the wind,
but you can see
leaves and grasses
shiver as it moves through them.

Scientists who study the weather
use a special machine which
measures the speed of the wind.
It is called an anemometer.
If the wind is blowing strongly
the cups spin round very quickly.

This also tells us something
about the wind.
The weather vane shows
the direction
from which the wind is blowing.

When the wind is blowing wildly
we say that the weather
is stormy.
Strong winds can uproot trees
and lift roofs off houses.

Some storms are very noisy.
Electricity builds up in
the storm clouds as they
move together.
The electricity must find its
way to earth.
You see it flash as lightning.
You hear it as thunder.

Sometimes there is no wind.
The air feels cool and damp.
When the weather is misty
you cannot see very far.
Road users must
take extra care.

In towns and cities,
smoke and fumes
from factories and cars
can become trapped
close to the ground.
This dirty air is called smog.

Scientists who study the weather
are called meteorologists.
They collect information
from weather stations…

and from satellites
flying high above the ground.
They use all the information
they collect
to prepare a weather forecast.

The forecast helps farmers
decide what work
can be done
in the fields…

and fishermen decide
whether to go out to sea.

The weather affects what we wear
and what we do.
Weather is important
to all living things.

But we cannot control
the weather.
What kind of weather
do you like best of all?

About this book

Young children acquire much information in an incidental, almost random fashion. Indeed, they learn much just by being alive! The books in this series complement the way in which young children learn. Through photographs and a simple text the readers are encouraged to comment on the world in which they live.

To the young child, life is new and almost everything in the world is of interest. But interest alone is not enough. If a child is to grow intellectually this interest has to be harnessed and extended. This book adopts a well tried and successful method of achieving this end. By focusing upon a particular topic, it invites the reader firstly to look and then to question. The words and photographs provide a starting point for discussion. Discussion also involves listening. The adult who listens to the young reader's observations will quickly realise that children have a very real concern for the environmental issues that confront us all.

Children enjoy having information books read to them just as much as stories and poetry. The younger child may ignore the written words … pictures play an important part in learning, particularly if they encourage talk and visual discrimination.

Henry Pluckrose